HAL•LEONARD
INSTRUMENTAL
PLAY-ALONG

AUDIO
ACCESS
INCLUDED

PLAYBACK+
Speed • Pitch • Balance • Loop

Flute

THE GREATEST SHOWMAN

T0039478

Come Alive...2

From Now On..3

The Greatest Show 4

A Million Dreams 5

Never Enough...6

The Other Side 8

Rewrite the Stars 9

This Is Me 10

Tightrope..12

Audio Arrangements by Peter Deneff

To access audio visit:
www.halleonard.com/mylibrary
Enter Code
2970-4626-6225-0568

ISBN 978-1-5400-2840-2

HAL•LEONARD®
7777 W. BLUEMOUND RD. P.O. BOX 13819 MILWAUKEE, WI 53213

In Australia Contact:
Hal Leonard Australia Pty. Ltd.
4 Lentara Court
Cheltenham, Victoria, 3192 Australia
Email: ausadmin@halleonard.com.au

Visit Hal Leonard Online at
www.halleonard.com

COME ALIVE

FLUTE

Words and Music by BENJ PASEK
and JUSTIN PAUL

FROM NOW ON

Flute

Words and Music by BENJ PASEK
and JUSTIN PAUL

THE GREATEST SHOW

Flute

Words and Music by BENJ PASEK,
JUSTIN PAUL and RYAN LEWIS

A MILLION DREAMS

FLUTE

Words and Music by BENJ PASEK
and JUSTIN PAUL

NEVER ENOUGH

FLUTE

Words and Music by BENJ PASEK
and JUSTIN PAUL

THE OTHER SIDE

Flute

Words and Music by BENJ PASEK
and JUSTIN PAUL

REWRITE THE STARS

FLUTE

Words and Music by BENJ PASEK
and JUSTIN PAUL

THIS IS ME

FLUTE

Words and Music by BENJ PASEK
and JUSTIN PAUL

11

TIGHTROPE

FLUTE

Words and Music by BENJ PASEK
and JUSTIN PAUL